NANCY BURNETT
Divorce What You Need to Know
A Lawyer's Easy-to-Follow Guide to Understanding Divorce

Copyright © 2024 by Nancy Burnett

All rights reserved. No part of this publication may be reproduced, stored or transmitted in any form or by any means, electronic, mechanical, photocopying, recording, scanning, or otherwise without written permission from the publisher. It is illegal to copy this book, post it to a website, or distribute it by any other means without permission.

First edition

This book was professionally typeset on Reedsy. Find out more at reedsy.com

Contents

Introduction	1
Chapter 1: Preliminaries and Prerequisites	2
Chapter 2: Child Custody	8
Chapter 3: Child Support and Alimony	31
Chapter 4: Property Division	37
Chapter 5: Restoration of Prior Name	39
Chapter 6: Attorneys	40
Glossary	44

Introduction

Divorce. It's a word that evokes a spectrum of emotions – grief, anger, confusion, and often, a sense of being adrift. If you're facing the prospect of divorce, you're likely feeling overwhelmed by the legal complexities that lie ahead. This book is your life raft in these uncharted waters.

I understand that the legal system surrounding divorce can feel like a foreign language. This comprehensive guide cuts through the legalese, providing clear and concise explanations of the key legal issues you'll encounter. From child custody and property division to alimony (also called spousal maintenance or spousal support) and more, I'll break down the law in a way that's easy to understand.

Also, although I am a Georgia attorney and my examples are based on my understanding of Georgia law, I have provided ample links to information for readers from other states.

Most importantly, this book empowers you. It will educate you about the core information you need to know if you are facing a divorce. It is not intended to replace your attorney but to provide a foundation of knowledge that your attorney can build upon.

Note: This book does not create an attorney-client relationship with me and does not constitute legal advice.

Chapter 1: Preliminaries and Prerequisites

Divorce is the legal process that ends a marriage. It untangles the legal ties between spouses, allowing them to be single again. In most cases, a court will oversee the divorce, dividing property and debts fairly, and if there are children, determine child custody and support arrangements. Divorce can be a complex emotional and legal experience, but it is a way for couples who can no longer live together to formally separate their lives. According to the Centers for Disease Control (www.cdc.gov), there were a total of 673,989 divorces in the 45 reporting states and D.C. in 2022. You are not alone.

Residency Requirements

Residency requirements are a hurdle you'll need to clear before filing for divorce in most states. These rules ensure a court has the authority to handle your case. Typically, one spouse must be a resident of the state for a set period, often six months to a year, right before filing. This establishes the court's jurisdiction over the marriage. Even if you both currently live elsewhere, if one spouse meets the residency requirement, you might be able to file in that state. In Georgia, you or your spouse (if you live in another state) must have been a resident of the state for six months before the petition for divorce is filed or, if you are not a resident but live on a military base, you can petition for divorce after a year. Thanks to Divorcenet.com, the residency requirement for each state can be found at www.divorcenet.com/resources/basic-divorce-residency-requirements-in-your-state.html.

Grounds (Reasons) for Divorce

When a court ends a marriage, there must be a reason for the divorce called "grounds." Some states have "no-fault grounds" in which a court can divorce parties without blame. Other states retain traditional divorce grounds such as adultery and abuse. Some states, like Georgia, have no-fault and fault grounds for divorce. The grounds for divorce authorized in Georgia are:

- The parties are too closely related.
- Mental incapacity at the time of the marriage.
- Impotency at the time of the marriage.
- Force, menace, duress, or fraud in obtaining the marriage.
- Pregnancy of the wife by a man other than the husband, at the time of the marriage, unknown to the husband.
- Adultery of either party after marriage.
- Willful and continued desertion by either of the parties for the term of one year.
- The conviction of either party for an offense involving moral turpitude (behavior that is below what is generally accepted in the community), under which that party is sentenced to prison for two or more years.
- Habitual intoxication.
- Cruel treatment such as reasonably justifies fear for life, limb or health and includes both mental and physical pain that is willfully committed.
- Incurable mental illness when certain criteria are met.
- Habitual drug addiction.
- The marriage is irretrievably broken.

For the grounds for divorce in your state, see www.divorcenet.com/topics/grounds-for-divorce.

If you live in a state that has fault and no-fault grounds for a divorce, you and your attorney can discuss the strategy of basing your divorce on fault, no-fault or both fault and no-fault grounds.

Immediate Rules You Must Follow

When a divorce begins, there may be statutes, rules of court or standing orders setting forth certain things you must do and certain things you may not do. For example, in my area of Georgia, there is a standing order requiring parties to civil actions (including domestic relations matters) participate in mediation. Also, O.C.G.A. §19-5-7 provides that property cannot be transferred during a divorce except a bona fide transfer in payment of preexisting debt. Finally, in my judicial circuit, all parties in cases where the interests of children are involved must complete the Seminar for Divorcing Parents. It is very important to ask your attorney about the rules that apply to you.

Litigation and Alternative Dispute Resolution

CHAPTER 1: PRELIMINARIES AND PREREQUISITES

Dispute resolution is the process of addressing a disagreement or argument so that it is resolved. The traditional method of dispute resolution is litigation. Litigation is the process of resolving a dispute in a court of law. Resolving matters in court is usually time-consuming and expensive. In family matters involving children where the parties must co-parent after the divorce, the litigation method is often harsh and leads to hurt or angry feelings that survive the divorce.

This brings us to alternative dispute resolution (ADR). In contrast to the adversarial nature of court battles, ADR offers a collaborative approach to resolving conflicts. One prominent form of ADR is mediation, where a neutral third party, the mediator, facilitates communication between disagreeing parties. Unlike a judge who imposes a decision, the mediator guides the conversation, helping each side understand the other's perspective and underlying interests. This fosters a space for creative solutions that address both parties' needs leading to a more satisfying outcome than a court-mandated ruling. It tends to reduce the cost of resolving the dispute and preserve the dignity of the parties who are now able to decide their own fate.

John and Sharon

John and Sharon Smith are examples we will use throughout this book.

John and Sharon met in Atlanta when John was 20 and Sharon was 19. When they met, John was studying biology at Georgia State University and Sharon was studying accounting. Sharon got pregnant with their oldest child prior to the marriage and John quit college to work and support her and the child. Sharon stayed in college and finished her degree.

They have been unhappy in their marriage. Neither party was cruel to the other party or committed adultery. But they have been arguing a lot and no amount of effort by them or counseling has resolved their difficulties. The family environment has become toxic. Sharon wants a divorce.

They own a house that was purchased during the marriage. It is worth $225,000 and there is a mortgage it secures which has a pay-off balance of $100,000. John inherited a rental property prior to marriage. Sharon's parents gave her a car during the marriage. John drives a car the parties bought during the marriage.

John and Sharon have three children: Amy is 15 and wants to live with her father; John, Jr. is 11 and wants to live with his mother. Sarah is 6 and her parents do not think she is old enough to decide where she wants to live.

About five years ago, Sharon was offered a great opportunity to work at the job of her dreams. Unfortunately, the job required travel five days a week and kept her out until 10 or 11 pm on most weeknights. The job came with a substantial pay increase. John and Sharon agreed that John would leave his job and take care of the home and children. Sharon's hours are more reasonable now and she is home shortly after 5 pm most nights.

Sharon now earns $180,000 per year. John receives $12,000 per year rental income from the house he inherited and pays $600 a year for insurance for the house and $1,000 per year for taxes.

Chapter 2: Child Custody

It is helpful to start a conversation about child custody by defining a few terms (which may vary from state to state so be sure to ask your attorney about that):

Legal custody: The person with legal custody of a child makes the major decisions for that child such as the child's religion, education, health and extracurricular activities.

<u>Joint legal custody</u>: Joint legal custody means that the parties shall share the major decision-making necessary for raising a child such as the child's religion, education, health and extracurricular activities.<u>Physical custody</u>: Physical care of a child. The child lives with the primary physical custodian. He or she visits or has parenting time with the other parent who may be referred to as the secondary custodian or the noncustodial parent.

<u>Joint physical custody</u>: Parties who share the care of their child equally or nearly equally have joint physical custody of the child.

Best Interests Standard

No custody discussion is complete without talking about the best interests of the child standard. In child custody cases, the "best interests of the child" standard is the guiding principle. This means all decisions about custody and visitation prioritize the child's well-being. Judges consider various factors like the child's safety, emotional ties to each parent, and the stability of each home environment. Ultimately, the goal is to create a custody arrangement that best supports the child's healthy development.

To determine the best interests of the child, judges of each state consider that state's set of factors. In Georgia, this set of factors is:

- The love, affection, bonding, and emotional ties existing between each parent and the child;
- The love, affection, bonding, and emotional ties existing between the child and his or her siblings, half siblings, and stepsiblings and the residence of such other children;
- The capacity and disposition of each parent to give the child love, affection, and guidance and to continue the education and rearing of the child;

- Each parent's knowledge and familiarity of the child and the child's needs;
- The capacity and disposition of each parent to provide the child with food, clothing, medical care, day-to-day needs, and other necessary basic care, with consideration made for the potential payment of child support by the other parent;
- The home environment of each parent considering the promotion of nurturance and safety of the child rather than superficial or material factors;
- The importance of continuity in the child's life and the length of time the child has lived in a stable, satisfactory environment and the desirability of maintaining continuity;
- The stability of the family unit of each of the parents and the presence or absence of each parent's support systems within the community to benefit the child;
- The mental and physical health of each parent, except to the extent as provided in Code Section 30-4-5 and this paragraph and such factors as provided in Code Section 15-11-26;
- Each parent's involvement, or lack thereof, in the child's educational, social, and extracurricular activities;
- Each parent's employment schedule and the related flexibility or limitations, if any, of a parent to care for the child;
- The home, school, and community record and history of the child, as well as any health or educational special needs of the child;
- Each parent's past performance and relative abilities for future performance of parenting responsibilities;
- The willingness and ability of each of the parents to facilitate and encourage a close and continuing parent-child relationship between the child and the other parent, consistent with the best interest of the child;
- Any recommendation by a court appointed custody evaluator or

guardian ad litem;
- Any evidence of family violence or sexual, mental, or physical child abuse or criminal history of either parent; and
- Any evidence of substance abuse by either parent.

For anyone facing a custody dispute, it is important to know the factors in your state. I have posted links below for your convenience.

- Alabama - Attorney John M. Totten has posted the factors considered in Alabama at https://johntottenlaw.com/6-key-factors-alabama-courts-consider-child-custody-cases/.
- Alaska - In Alaska, the factors are posted on the website for the courts at www.courts.alaska.gov/shc/family/shcparenting.htm#factors.
- Arizona - Hildebrand Law has posted the factors for Arizona at https://hildebrandlaw.com/child-custody-laws laws -in-arizona-2/child-custody-factors-arizona/.
- Arkansas – Thanks to the Sheppard Firm, we have the factors for Arkansas at https://oliviasheppardlaw.com/blog/how-is-custody-decided-in-arkansas/.
- California – San Diego Divorce Lawyers, APC has posted the factors for California at www.sachdevfamilylaw.com/blog/6-factors-that-affect-child-custody-decisions-in-california/.
- Colorado – The factors for Colorado are posted by Robinson & Henry, P.C. at www.robinsonandhenry.com/colorado/family-law/child-custody-in-colorado/#stepthree.
- Connecticut - www.mcconnellfamilylaw.com/connecticut-courts-consider-ruling-child-custody/#the-best-interests-of-the-children has the factors for Connecticut thanks to the McConnell Family Law Group.
- Delaware – Family Court of the State of Delaware has posted its

factors at https://courts.delaware.gov/forms/download.aspx?id=30208.
- Florida – Thanks to Grant J. Gisondo, P.A., we have the factors for Florida posted at https://gisondolaw.com/fla-stat-61-13-child-custody-factors/.
- Idaho – The Idaho State Bar has posted these factors at https:\\isb.idaho.gov/ilf/wp-content/uploads/sites/2/CHILD-CUSTODY-UNDER-IDAHO-LAW.pdf.
- Illinois – The factors have been posted at www.oflaherty-law.com/learn-about-law/types-of-evidence-and-relevant-factors-in-child-custody-cases-in-illinois by Kevin O'Flaherty.
- Indiana – McNevin and McInnes, PC. has posted the factors for Indiana at www.indyadvocate.com/8-factors-that-can-determine-child-custody-in-indiana/.
- Iowa – Eugene Nassif with O'Flaherty Law wrote an article about child custody including these factors for Iowa which can be found at www.oflaherty-law.com/learn-about-law/iowa-child-custody-guide.
- Kansas – The factors for Kansas are at www.hamptonlaw.com/blog/child-custody-in-kansas/ thanks to Russel B. Prophet of Hampton & Royce, L.C.
- Kentucky – At www.hoffmanlawyer.com/practice-areas/child-custody-attorney-florence-ky/, Hoffman, Walker & Knauf have posted the factors for Kentucky.
- Louisiana – Friley & Dugas, LLC say that there are four main factors that the courts there consider. See, www.kfrileylaw.com/blog/2023/06/4-main-factors-used-in-child-custody-determinations-in-louisiana/.
- Maine – These factors for Maine are posted by the State of Maine Judicial Branch at www.courts.maine.gov/courts/family/divorce-separation/decisions-children.html.

CHAPTER 2: CHILD CUSTODY

- Maryland – You can find Maryland's factors at www.peoples-law.org/child-custody-maryland#best-interest posted by The People's Law Library of Maryland.
- Massachusetts – Miller Law Group, P.C. has posted the factors for Massachusetts at www.apmillerlawgroup.com/blog/2015/may/how-do-judges-decide-child-custody-in-massachuse/.
- Michigan – The factors for Michigan have been posted at www.courts.michigan.gov/4a7b4e/siteassets/court-administration/standardsguidelines/foc/custodyguideline.pdf by the Michigan courts.
- Minnesota – Thanks to Terzich & Ort, LLP the guidelines for Minnesota can be found at www.tolawoffice.com/divorce-in-minnesota/child-custody/what-are-the-12-best-interest-factors-in-child-custody/.
- Mississippi – Vic Carmody, Jr. P.A. has posted the factors for Mississippi at www.mississippi-lawyers.com/blog/mississippis-albright-factors-for-child-custody-what-is-in-the-childs-best-interest/. Interestingly, the factors in Mississippi do not come from a statute but from a court case.
- Missouri – A shout out to The Betz Law Firm for posting Missouri's factors at https:\\betzlawfirm.com/8-factors-that-determine-child-custody-in-missouri/.
- Montana – Gravis Law has posted these factors for Montana at https://gravislaw.com/family-law/understanding-child-custody-determination-in-montana-family-law/.
- Nebraska – The factors for Nebraska are at the Nebraska Legal Group's website at
- www.nebraskalegalgroup.com/child-custody-in-nebraska/child-custody-faqs/Nevada – Molly Rosenblum has posted the factors for Nevada at www.rosenblumlawlv.com/nevada-child-custody-laws/.

- New Hampshire – The factors for New Hampshire are discussed at www.cindyclarklaw.com/articles/5-factors-a-new-hampshire-judge-considers-in-child-custody-cases/ thanks to Clark Law, PLLC.
- New Jersey – The Edens Law Group has provided the factors for New Jersey at https://edens-law.com/behind-the-gavel-understanding-the-factors-that-determine-child-custody-in-new-jersey/.
- New Mexico – In New Mexico, the factors are listed by Advanced Legal Resolutions at www.nmfamilylawyer.com/understanding-new-mexico-child-custody-laws.
- New York – New York City's Bar has posted New York's factors at www.nycbar.org/get-legal-help/article/family-law/child-custody-and-parenting-plans/best-interests-of-the-child/.
- North Carolina – Thanks to Blood Law, PLLC we have the factors for North Carolina at www.blood-law.com/blog/2022/september/north-carolina-child-custody-basics/.
- North Dakota – Fremstad Law has provided the North Dakota factors at www.fremstadlaw.com/factors-in-north-dakota-child-custody/.
- Ohio – The factors (or criteria) for Ohio are provided by Cathy R. Cook at www.cathycooklaw.com/wp-content/uploads/2021/02/child-custody-report.pdf.
- Oklahoma – At https://oklaw.org/resource/child-custody-unwed-parents we have the factors for Oklahoma under the section "Custody and Visitation Considerations" which must be clicked on for the list to drop down for you to read.
- Oregon – The Oregon Judicial Branch has posted their factors at www.courts.oregon.gov/programs/family/children/Pages/custody-parenting-time.aspx under the tab "Factors a Judge Will Consider."

CHAPTER 2: CHILD CUSTODY

- Pennsylvania – Thanks to Colgan & Associates there is a list of the factors judge in Pennsylvania use to determine custody at www.cmlaw1.com/16-factors-determine-custody/.
- Rhode Island – Bilodeau Capalbo, LLC has posted the factors list for Rhode Island at www.bilodeaucapalbo.com/blog/the-factors-rhode-island-courts-consider-when-making-child-custody-determinations/.
- South Carolina – We can thank Futeral & Nelson, LLC for their website at https://charlestonlaw.net/custody-laws-south-carolina/ which provides the factors for South Carolina.
- South Dakota – At www.sdlawhelp.org/node/49/custody-visitation, SD Law Help has provided the factors for South Dakota.
- Tennessee – The factors used by Tennssee courts has been provided by LaFevor Slaughter at www.jameslafevor.com/factors-tennessee-child-custody-decisions/.
- Texas – The factors for Texas are at https://texaslawhelp.org/article/best-interest-of-the-child-standard thanks to TexasLawHelp.org.
- Utah – The law firm of Pearson Butler has provided the Utah factors at www.pearsonbutler.com/blog/2024/march/understanding-child-custody-laws/.
- Vermont – Legal Lead Solutions, LLC has provided these factors for Vermont at www.familylawrights.net/vermont/child-custody/.
- Virginia – The factors a Virginia judge must consider can be found at https://hoflaw.com/blog/10-factors-you-must-consider-in-your-virginia-child-custody-case/ courtesy of Hofheimer Family Law Firm.
- Washington – For Washington readers, Clement Law Center provided the factors at www.clementlawcenter.com/blog/2016/09/the-factors-considered-in-a-washington-custody-case/.
- West Virginia – From my review, it appears that West Virginia

changed its law to create a presumption in favor of equal 50/50 custody (see, for example, https://legalaidwv.org/news/navigating-west-virginias-new-custody-law/). This presumption can be rebutted (disputed) and, if so, it appears that some factors come into play. These factors are generally explained at the same URL.
- Wisconsin – First Look Family Law has posted the factors for our Wisconsin readers at https://firstlookfamilylaw.com/what-does-the-best-interest-of-the-child-mean-in-a-wisconsin-custody-case/.
- Wyoming – The factors for Wyoming have been provided by Legal Aid of Wyoming at https://lawyoming.org/blog/child-custody-the-basics.

Parenting Plans

In Georgia, all divorcing parents are required to prepare a Parenting Plan. This Parenting Plan can be a plan proposed by either party where custody is in dispute, prepared jointly or determined by the Court.

John and Sharon's Parenting Plan.

John and Sharon want to respect the wishes of their older children about where the children wish to live (Amy with John and John, Jr. with Sharon). In Georgia, as in many states, courts can consider the wishes of the child in making custody decisions. Georgia children who are 14 or older have the right to select the parent with whom he or she desires to live, and that selection shall be presumptive unless placement with the preferred parent would not be in the best interests of the child. In cases where the child is 11 or older but less than 14, the judge shall consider the desires and educational needs of the child in determining which parent shall have custody. See www.custodyxchange.com/topics/research/custody-preferences-children.php for a state-by-state guide about the applicability a child's wishes about where to live have on the ultimate custody decision.

Note that Amy will reside with John while John, Jr. will reside with Sharon. This is called split custody. Courts usually disfavor separating siblings but will do so in some cases such as where an older child has a preference or where siblings have such a conflict-filled relationship that is best to separate them (such as where one sibling abuses the other).

John and Sharon agree that their youngest child, Sarah, will spend equal time with both parents (joint physical custody). She will follow a week on/week off arrangement.

The parties want to maintain the sibling bonds among their children. They have decided that the children will spend their weekends and vacations together. The mother will have the children on alternating weekends and holidays assigned to her and the father will have them on alternating weekends and holidays assigned to him.

John and Sharon agree that they will share decision-making about the children (joint legal custody). If they cannot agree about a decision, Sharon will make the final decision about educational and religious upbringing issues and John will make the final decision about non-emergency health care and extracurricular activities.

One of my favorite websites to help parents communicate with each other, Our Family Wizard, has a checklist to help parents write a parenting plan at www.ourfamilywizard.com/blog/checklist-writing-parenting-plan. Be sure to discuss this with your attorney before you commit yourself to any decision.

Since John and Sharon have an agreement about custody and visitation, they have jointly prepared a Parenting Plan (see below):

PARENTING PLAN

(X) The parties have agreed to the terms of this plan and this information has been furnished by both parties to meet the requirements of OCGA §19-9-1. The parties agree on the terms of the plan and affirm the accuracy of the information provided, as shown by their signatures at the end of this order.

( ) This plan has been prepared by the Judge.

This plan
   (X) is a new plan.
   ( ) modifies an existing Parenting Plan dated _____.
   ( ) modifies an existing Order dated _____.

Child's Name Year of Birth

Amy Smith 2009
  John Smith, Jr. 2013
  Sarah Smith 2018

Custody and Decision Making

Legal Custody shall be (choose one:)
   ( ) with the Mother
   ( ) with the Father
   (X) Joint

Primary Physical Custodian

For each of the children named below the primary physical custodian shall be:

CHAPTER 2: CHILD CUSTODY

Amy Smith y/o/b: 2009 ( ) Mother (X) Father ( ) Joint
  John Smith, Jr. y/o/b: 2013 (X) Mother ( ) Father ( ) Joint
  Sarah Smith y/o/b: 2018 ( ) Mother ( ) Father (X) Joint

WHERE JOINT PHYSICAL CUSTODY IS CHOSEN BY THE PARENTS OR ORDERED BY THE COURT, A DETAILED PLAN OF THE LIVING ARRANGEMENTS OF THE CHILD(REN) SHALL BE ATTACHED AND MADE A PART OF THIS PARENTING PLAN.

Day-to-Day Decisions

Each parent shall make decisions regarding the day-to-day care of a child while the child is residing with that parent, including any emergency decisions affecting the health or safety of a child.

Major decisions regarding each child shall be made as follows:

Educational Decisions ( ) Mother ( ) Father (X) Joint
  Non-emergency Health Care ( ) Mother ( ) Father (X) Joint
  Religious Upbringing ( ) Mother ( ) Father (X) Joint
  Extracurricular Activities ( ) Mother ( ) Father (X) Joint

Disagreements

Where parents have elected joint decision making above, please explain how any disagreements in decision-making will be resolved:

The parties shall first consult with one another before making any major non-emergency decision. After consulting with one another, then and only then shall the father make the final decision concerning Amy Smith, the mother shall make the final decision concerning John Smith, Jr. and the mother shall make the final decision concerning Sarah Smith if it is an educational or extracurricular activity matter and the father shall make the final decision concerning Sarah Smith if it is a non-emergency health care or religious upbringing issue.

Parenting Time/Visitation Schedules
Parenting Time/Visitation

During the term of this parenting plan the non-custodial parent shall have at a minimum the following rights of parenting time/visitation (choose an item):

( ) The weekend of the first and third Friday of each month.

( ) The weekend of the first, third, and fifth Friday of each month.

( ) The weekend of the second and fourth Friday of each month.

( ) Every other weekend starting on _____.

( ) Each _____ starting at _____ a.m./p.m. and ending _____ a.m./p.m.

(X) Other: The children shall all visit the parents on alternating weekends from Friday at 6:00 pm until Sunday at 6:00 pm. Sarah Smith shall spend a week with her mother then a week with her father, repeating this schedule indefinitely. Sarah Smith shall be exchanged on Sundays at 6:00 pm.

( ) and weekday parenting time/visitation on (choose an item):
  ( ) None
  ( ) Every Wednesday evening
  ( ) Every other Wednesday during the week prior to a non-visitation weekend.

CHAPTER 2: CHILD CUSTODY

( ) Every _____ and _____ evening.
( ) Other:

For purposes of this parenting plan, a weekend will start at 6:00 p.m. on Friday and end at 6:00 p.m. on Sunday.

Weekday visitation will begin at _____ a.m./p.m. and will end _____ a.m./p.m./when the child(ren) return(s) to school or day care the next morning/Other: _____].

This parenting schedule begins:

( ) _____ (day and time) OR (X) date of the Court's Order

Major Holidays and Vacation Periods

Thanksgiving

The day to day schedule shall apply unless other arrangements are set forth:

The father shall have parenting time with the children for the Thanksgiving Holidays in even numbered years and the mother shall have parenting time with the children for the Thanksgiving Holidays in odd numbered years. Thanksgiving Holidays begin the day and time school is released for the holiday until 6:00 pm the evening before school resumes.
    beginning _____.

Winter Vacation

The (X) mother ( ) father shall have the child(ren) for the first period from the day and time school is dismissed until December 26th at 6:00

p.m. in ( ) odd numbered years (X) even numbered years ( ) every year. The other parent will have the child(ren) for the second period from the day and time indicated above until 6:00 p.m. on the evening before school resumes. Unless otherwise indicated, the parties shall alternate the first and second periods each year.

Other agreement of the parents:

Summer Vacation

Define summer vacation period: from Sunday following the day the children are released from school for the holiday at 6:00 pm until the Sunday before school resumes after the holiday at 6:00 pm.

The day-to-day schedule shall apply unless other arrangements are set forth:
    The children shall alternate weeks with their parents on the same schedule Sarah Smith follows.
    beginning the Sunday after school is released for the summer.

Spring Vacation (if applicable)

Define: From the day and time school is released for the holiday until 6:00 p.m. the evening before school resumes.

The day-to-day schedule shall apply unless other arrangements are set forth:
    The Mother shall have this vacation period with the children in odd numbered years and the Father shall have this vacation period in even numbered years.
    beginning the day and time school is released for the holiday the next

Spring Vacation.

Other Holiday Schedule (if applicable)

Mother Father

Martin Luther King Day Even years Odd years
    Presidents' Day
    Mother's Day Every year
    Memorial Day Odd years Even years
    Father's Day Every year
    July Fourth Even years Odd years
    Labor Day Even years Odd years
    Halloween Odd years Even years
    Child(ren)'s Birthday(s) Even years Odd years
    Mother's Birthday Every year
    Father's Birthday Every year
    Religious Holidays:

* * *

Other: _____ _____
    Other: _____ _____
    Other: _____ _____

Other extended periods of time during school, etc. (refer to the school schedule)

Start and end dates for holiday visitation

For the purposes of this parenting plan, the holiday will start and end as follows (choose one):

(X) Holidays that fall on Friday will include the following Saturday and Sunday
   (X) Holidays that fall on Monday will include the preceding Saturday and Sunday
   ( ) Other: _____

Coordination of Parenting Schedules

Check if applicable:

(X) The holiday parenting time/visitation schedule takes precedence over the regular parenting time/visitation schedule.

( ) When the child(ren) is/are with a parent for an extended parenting time/visitation period (such as summer), the other parent shall be entitled to visit with the child(ren) during the extended period, as follows:

1. **Transportation Arrangements**

For visitation, the place of meeting for the exchange of the child(ren) shall be:

The parties shall exchange the children at the parking lot of the Walmart on Shugart Road in Dalton, GA.

CHAPTER 2: CHILD CUSTODY

The _____ will be responsible for the transportation of the child(ren) at the beginning of visitation.

The _____ will be responsible for the transportation of the child(ren) at the conclusion of visitation.

Transportation costs, if any, will be allocated as follows:

* * *

* * *

Other provisions: _____

Contacting the Child(ren)

When the child(ren) is/are in the physical custody of one parent, the other parent will have the right to contact the child(ren) as follows:

(X) Telephone

(X) Other: Via videochat and mail

( ) Limitations on contact:

Supervision of Parenting Time (if applicable)

( ) Check here if applicable

Supervised parenting time shall apply to the day-to-day schedule as follows:

Place: _____

Person/Organization supervising: _____

Responsibility for cost:

( ) Mother ( ) Father ( ) Both equally

Communication Provisions

(X) Each parent shall promptly notify the other parent of a change of address, phone number or cell phone number. A parent changing residence must give at least 30 days' notice of the change and provide the full address of the new residence.

( ) Due to prior acts of family violence, the address of the child(ren) and victim of family violence shall be kept confidential. The protected party shall promptly notify the other parent, through a third party, of any change in contact information necessary to conduct visitation.

Access to Records and Information

CHAPTER 2: CHILD CUSTODY

Absent agreement to limitations or court ordered limitations, pursuant to O.C.G.A. §19-9-1 (b) (1) (D), both parents are entitled to access to all of the child(ren)'s records and information including, but not limited to, education, health, extracurricular activities, and religious communications. Designation as a non-custodial parent does not affect a parent's right to equal access to these records.

Limitations on Access Rights:
  Other Information Sharing Provisions:

* * *

* * *

* * *

The parents shall notify one another if a child misses school for any reason and shall notify one another of any health care appointments or treatment. If a child is injured, the parents shall notify one another and explain the circumstances.

Modification of Plan or Disagreements

Parties may, by mutual agreement, vary the parenting time/visitation; however, such agreement shall not be a binding court order. Custody shall only be modified by court order.

Should the parents disagree about this parenting plan or wish to modify

Special Considerations

Please attach an addendum detailing any special circumstances of which the Court should be aware (e.g., health issues, educational issues, etc.).

Parents' Consent

Please review the following and initial:

We recognize that a close and continuing parent-child relationship and continuity in the child's life is in the child's best interest.

Mother's Initials: _____ Father's Initials: _____

We recognize that our child's needs will change and grow as the child matures; we have made a good faith effort

Mother's Initials: _____ Father's Initials: _____

We recognize that the parent with physical custody will make the day-to-day decisions and emergency decisions while the child is residing with such parent.

Mother's Initials: _____ Father's Initials: _____

(X) We knowingly and voluntarily agree on the terms of this Parenting Plan. Each of us affirms that the information we have provided in this Plan is true and correct.

_____

Mother's Signature

_____

Father's Signature

Chapter 6: Attorneys

If you and your soon-to-be ex-spouse have been unable to come up with an agreement on custody/visitation issues, you really *need* to talk to an attorney. Child custody litigation is complicated and difficult. Also, you are not likely to be objective about this when it comes to your child.

In a custody case, the Court might appoint a Guardian ad litem (GAL), an advocate whose primary responsibility is to represent the best interests of a child in legal proceedings, particularly in cases involving custody disputes, abuse, neglect, or other matters affecting the child's welfare. GALs are typically attorneys with expertise in child development, family dynamics, and relevant legal procedures. They may conduct thorough investigations, including interviews with the child, parents, caregivers, schools, doctors and other involved parties, to gather information about the child's circumstances. Based on their findings, GALs provide recommendations to the court regarding custody arrangements, visitation schedules, and other matters pertaining to the child's care. Their role is to ensure that the child's voice is heard and their interests are adequately represented within the legal process, serving as their advocate throughout the proceedings. In New York, although this state has GALs, this role is often filled by a Law Guardian GAL.

In a contested case, the parties and the children may be required to go through a psychological evaluation. In cases of substance abuse allegations, a parent might be required to take a drug test or undergo a substance abuse evaluation. You can expect extensive discovery in a contested custody case, too. Discovery is a phase of the case where the parties exchange information and documents.

Chapter 3: Child Support and Alimony

Before we talk about child support (money one parent pays to the other for maintenance of the child) and alimony (money one spouse pays to the other for that spouse's maintenance), it is important to talk about financial disclosure. In addition to whatever else may be required of you, you can expect that you will be required to disclose your income, expenses, assets and liabilities (debts). In Georgia, the form for this is a Domestic Relations Affidavit (sometimes called a DRFA). Georgia's form is posted on the internet at www.cherokeega.com/Clerk-of-Courts/resources/documents/Financialaffidavit.pdf. Other states have their own form for disclosing income, expenses, assets and debts.

Turning to Georgia's form, you will see that several forms of income are considered in "gross income" including salaries, commissions, fees, tips, self-employment income, bonuses, overtime payments, severance pay, recurring income from pensions or retirement plans, interest income, dividend income, income from a trust, income from annuities, capital gains, disability or retirement benefits received from the Social Security Administration, veteran's disability benefits, workers' compensation benefits, unemployment insurance benefits, judgments recovered for personal injuries and awards from other civil actions gifts that consist of cash or other liquid instruments (or can be converted to cash), prizes, lottery winnings, alimony or maintenance received from persons other than the parties, assets which are used for the support of the family and other income. Fringe benefits a parent receives can be included as income if the benefits significantly reduce personal living expenses. For military members, income includes base pay, drill pay, basic allowance for subsistence, and basic allowance for housing. The following are *not* income for child support purposes in Georgia:

- Child support payments received by either parent for the benefit of a child of another relationship;
- Benefits received from means-tested public assistance programs such as, but not limited to:
- PeachCare for Kids Program, Temporary Assistance for Needy Families Program, or similar programs in other states or territories under Title IV-A of the federal Social Security Act;
- Food stamps or the value of food assistance provided by way of electronic benefits transfer procedures by the Department of Human Services;
- Supplemental security income received under Title XVI of the federal Social Security Act;
- Benefits received from Social Security Act disabled adult children of deceased disabled workers; and
- Low-income heating and energy assistance program payments;
- Foster care payments paid by the Department of Human Services or a licensed child-placing agency for providing foster care to a foster child in the custody of the Department of Human Services;
- A nonparent custodian's gross income; and
- Benefits received under Title IV-B or IV-E of the federal Social Security Act and state funding associated therewith for adoption assistance.

Once income is determined, there are various additions and subtractions for:

- Self-employment tax
- Preexisting child support orders
- Other children in the home
- Health insurance premiums
- Childcare expenses

Once the gross income minus or plus the above adjustments are made, your attorney will calculate your presumptive child support obligation using the child support calculator which is online. This is the amount that should be ordered in your case if you do not qualify for a deviation. Deviations are upward or downward adjustments to the presumptive child support amount to arrive at a final child support calculator. Deviations in Georgia are:

- High income
- Low Income
- Other health related insurance
- Life insurance
- Child and dependent care tax credit
- Visitation-related travel expenses
- Alimony
- Mortgage
- Permanency plan or foster care plan
- Extraordinary expenses
- Parenting time
- Nonspecific deviations

Once child support is determined, if the parent receives Social Security and the child receives a check on the parent's account, the check the child receives on the parent's account can be applied to reduce or eliminate the final child support amount in Georgia.

Child Support Calculators

Georgia has its child support calculator online at https://csconlinecalc.georgiacourts.gov/frontend/web/index.php. The links for all states' child support calculators is at https://hellodivorce.com/parenting/child-support-calculators-for-every-state. While you can use these calculators to consider various options, it is best to consult with your attorney about child support.

John and Sharon – In determining their incomes, Sharon's was simply $180,000 per year divided by 12 months or $15,000 per month. John's income is $12,000 per year but he must pay $1,000 for taxes and $600 per year for insurance. Subtracting these legitimate expenses necessary to produce the income, John's net income is $10,400 per year or $866.67 per month. Plugging these incomes into the child support worksheet together with the information about the children and the parties and the worksheet shows that the amount of child support Sharon would pay John for one child is $1,584.

This is a split custody case, so a child support calculation must be made for each child. The parties have joint physical custody of Sarah, so a third worksheet must be done for her. Because there are awards going both directions, the child support amounts should be netted until a final child support award is determined.

In John and Sharon's case, the child support award to John for Amy would be $1,584 per month. The child support award to Sharon for John, Jr. would be $91.46 per month (from the child support worksheet). Netting these two figures results in an amount of child support for Amy and John, Jr. of $1,493 to be paid by Sharon to John.

This leaves the issue of child support for Sarah. Because she lives with both parents equal time, some people (even lawyers) believe that means that no child support has to be paid for her. That is a myth. The child support guidelines in Georgia require a calculation of the presumptive amount of child support for her ($1,584) and then the court can consider if it wants to deviate downwards. For most parents with similar income, no child support seems fair and would likely be allowed by the judge. But in a case like this, where one parent has substantially more income than the other, this may not be fair. Considering that their attorneys have told both John and Sharon that it is hard to predict what a judge might do with this situation, the parties decided to agree upon a downward deviation for Sarah of $800 leaving the net child support for Sarah to be paid by Sharon to John of $784. So, the final child support amount is $2,277 ($1,493 plus $784).

Alimony

In Georgia, a party who has committed adultery or desertion will not be granted alimony. In other situations, alimony might be granted. Unlike child support, alimony has no calculator that provides a presumptively correct amount that should be awarded. Instead, the Court considers the following factors in deciding whether to award alimony and how much to award:

- The standard of living established during the marriage;
- The duration of the marriage;
- The age and the physical and emotional condition of both parties;
- The financial resources of each party;
- Where applicable, the time necessary for either party to acquire

sufficient education or training to enable him to find appropriate employment;
- The contribution of each party to the marriage, including, but not limited to, services rendered in homemaking, child care, education, and career building of the other party;
- The condition of the parties, including the separate estate, earning capacity, and fixed liabilities of the parties; and
- Such other relevant factors as the court deems equitable and proper.

After considering all of these factors, the parties have decided that Sharon will pay John $1,500 per month in alimony for 7 years.

Modification of Orders

Support orders may be modified in certain cases. You may have to show that there has been a change of circumstances since the last order was made or you may find that your local child support enforcement agency (if you apply for their services) will conduct a review every certain number of years although you may have to request the review. You or your attorney can also petition the court to modify alimony or child support.

Chapter 4: Property Division

There are two main methods for dividing property in divorce across the United States: community property and equitable distribution. Each approaches marital assets and debts differently:

- **Community Property:** This system, in effect in nine states (Arizona, California, Idaho, Louisiana, Nevada, New Mexico, Texas, Washington, and Wisconsin), treats all property acquired during the marriage as jointly owned by both spouses. Debts incurred during the marriage are also considered shared liabilities. During divorce, the community property is simply divided equally, with each spouse receiving 50%. Separate property, assets owned by one spouse before the marriage or acquired through inheritance or gift from a third party during the marriage, generally remains with that spouse.
- **Equitable Distribution:** This method, used in the remaining states, focuses on a fair, but not necessarily equal, division of marital property. The court considers various factors to determine a just distribution, including:

Length of the marriage: Longer marriages tend to see a more equal split. **The value of each spouse's contribution:** This includes financial contributions like income and non-financial contributions like homemaking or childcare.

The separate property of each spouse: A spouse who might otherwise qualify for alimony might not receive alimony if he or she has substantial separate assets that can be used for her support.

The earning capacity of each spouse: The future financial situation of each spouse is factored in.

The needs of any children: The court might consider awarding the primary caregiver the marital home to ensure stability for the children.

Equitable distribution allows for more flexibility than community property, tailoring the division to the specific circumstances of the couple. However, it can also be a more complex and potentially contentious process, as there's no automatic 50/50 split.

Georgia is an equitable distribution state. In making property distributions here, we first classify the property of the parties into separate property and marital property. Marital property is property purchased by the parties during the marriage. Separate property is property that a party brought to the marriage and property acquired by gift or inheritance.

Classifying John and Sharon's property would result in a finding that the house and the car that John drives are marital property. The rental property John owned prior to marriage is separate property. Even if it had been acquired after the marriage, it would be separate property because it was inherited. The car Sharon drives is her separate property because her parents gave it to her.

Accordingly, Sharon gets her car and John gets his rental property. The parties have decided to sell the house and split the proceeds after the mortgage is paid. The parties agree that John can keep the car he drives.

Chapter 5: Restoration of Prior Name

Restoring you to your maiden or a prior surname is part of a divorce. Just be sure that there is language is in the final decree restoring you to your prior name if you want. When you get your copy of the judgment from the clerk of court, ask for a certified copy. This is necessary in some cases such as working with the Georgia Department of Driver Services and having one is worth a minimal fee.

Take the certified copy of your judgment to the driver's license agency for your state and ask them to change your name on your driver's license. After you receive your license, you should follow the instructions at www.ssa.gov/personal-record/change-name to see if you can get a social security card in your restored name online or must go to the nearest Social Security Administration office.

Don't forget to change your name at your doctor's and dentist's offices, your bank, your employer, your insurance agent(s), etc.

Chapter 6: Attorneys

You are not required to be represented by an attorney in a divorce but it is a good idea for several reasons:

- **Understanding Complexities:** Divorce law can be intricate. An attorney can navigate these complexities, ensuring you understand your rights and obligations throughout the process.
- **Protecting Your Assets:** Dividing marital property requires careful consideration. An attorney can help identify and value assets, including retirement accounts and investments. They can also ensure a fair and equitable division based on your state's laws (like equitable distribution in Georgia) and your specific circumstances.
- **Negotiating Favorable Terms:** Whether it's child custody arrangements, alimony, or property division, your attorney can represent your best interests during negotiations. Their experience and knowledge of the legal system can help you achieve a more favorable outcome.
- **Managing Emotional Strain:** Divorce can be emotionally charged, clouding judgment. An attorney can provide objective guidance and handle communication with your spouse's lawyer, reducing stress and allowing you to focus on moving forward.
- **Avoiding Costly Mistakes:** Trying to navigate the legal aspects of

divorce on your own can lead to mistakes that could cost you more in the long run. An attorney can help you avoid missing deadlines, filing incorrect paperwork, or unknowingly undervaluing assets.

Here are some additional situations where an attorney is strongly recommended:

- **High-conflict divorce:** If emotions are running high and communication with your spouse is strained, an attorney can act as a buffer and advocate for your needs.
- **Complex finances:** If you have significant assets, debts, or retirement accounts, an attorney can ensure a fair and accurate division.
- **Children involved:** Child custody arrangements are crucial and require careful consideration. An attorney can represent your interests and advocate for your children's well-being.
- **History of abuse:** If there has been domestic violence or abuse, legal protection and clear custody arrangements become even more important. An attorney can guide you through the legal process and ensure your safety.

How to Find an Attorney

Many people find an attorney by discussing their need for an attorney with someone who refers them to an attorney they know or have heard about. Other people find an attorney by searching online. Martindale (Martindale.com) has a database of attorneys with reviews from other attorneys and reviews from clients to help you choose an attorney. If you find an attorney you think might be appropriate, you can verify he or she is licensed and has no public disciplinary history from the bar association or, in some states, a court or state agency. In Georgia, you can find these details by searching the database at www.gabar.org. For other states, you can use the database at www.Martindale.com.

Working with an attorney – Your attorney and you have a unique and professional relationship. It is important that both of you respect each other and treat each other with courtesy. Some tips for working with an attorney:

- Show up for appointments and show up on time.
- Call your attorney during normal business hours unless there is an emergency that the attorney can address after hours or on weekends (there are not many of these).
- Keep a custody journal. It should be a journal just about custody. It should include the dates and times of each exchange of the children, note any problems with the exchange, document statements made by the other party, etc.
- Your attorney is not your therapist or emotional punching bag. During a divorce you may experience a wide range of emotions including sadness, despair, fear, anger, grief, guilt, impatience and more. Do not call your attorney and scream or otherwise verbally abuse the attorney.
- Be honest. An attorney cannot help you with only part of the information or with false information. In these circumstances, the client usually ends up with a bad result.

Attorney's Fees and Awards of Attorney's Fees

In my area, attorney fees range in the neighborhood of $200-$300 per hour or more. It is important to get the most of all the time you spend with your attorney to keep your legal fees to a minimum.

You can ask the court to make an award of attorney's fees to you (if

CHAPTER 6: ATTORNEYS

you already paid them) or your attorney. Ask your attorney if an award of attorney's fees would be appropriate in your case.

Throughout these pages, we have explored grounds for divorce, child custody, child support and alimony and more. As we draw to a close, I hope you have found this book helpful and enlightening and that it has supplemented your attorney's guidance. If your attorney disagrees with anything I have said in this book, follow your attorney's advice. He or she knows all the facts of your case, the laws in your state and the tendencies of the judges in the area to decide certain issues certain ways. Your attorney is in the best position to judge the best advice for you.

Glossary

Adjusted income: Means the determination of a party's income after deducting allowed expenses (for example, self-employment tax or child support orders for other children not part of this case).

Affidavit: An affidavit is a document signed by someone who is swearing that the document is true and complete. It is a criminal offense to lie on an affidavit.

Alimony: Alimony is payment of money by one spouse to the other spouse to support him or her temporarily or permanently.

Alternative dispute resolution (ADR): Any method of resolving a dispute that does not take place in a courtroom including negotiation, mediation and arbitration.

Annulment: The act of declaring a marriage invalid or void.

Arrears: Money that was supposed to be paid earlier and is still owed. It is used in the context of alimony and child support when the payor has fallen behind in payments.

GLOSSARY

Child support: Money paid to a custodial parent by a noncustodial parent for the support and maintenance of their child or children.

Complaint: The document that sets forth a party's claim against another party.

Contested divorce: A contested divorce is a divorce where one or both parties disagree with some aspect of the divorce.

Custodial parent: A parent who has been awarded sole physical custody or with whom the child primarily lives.

Decree: A court order.

Default: When the defendant/respondent does not answer the divorce petition (or complaint)

Defendant: The party who is being sued.

Deviation: In the context of child support guidelines, a deviation is an upward or downward adjustment in the amount of support due to specified factors such as low income, high income, parenting time, etc.

Discovery: In a divorce, discovery is that phase of the case where the parties exchange information and documents.

Domestic relations financial affidavit: Most states require parties to prepare and share a financial affidavit showing their income, expenses, assets and liabilities. In Georgia, this affidavit is called a Domestic Relations Financial Affidavit.

Equitable division: A process of dividing the property of a divorcing couple that takes into consideration various factors to determine what is fair to the parties. Contrary to popular belief, it is not equal division.

Ex parte: An extraordinary form of relief from the court where the court only considers one side of the dispute. It is typically used when a divorce is started to set temporary custody where there is cause to do so before the first court appearance, restraining orders and other matters.

Health insurance: Any general health or medical policy that pays doctors and other health care practitioners or reimburses the owner of the policy for medical expenses paid by the owner of the policy.

Income or gross income: Income is money that is coming in to a party such as money earned from a job, interest, dividends, rental income, etc. Gross income refers to income before expenses, such as taxes, are deducted.

Interrogatories: During discovery, one party may send a document to the other party (or his or her attorney) that requires that other party to answer questions listed on the document. These questions are called interrogatories.

Joint legal custody: Joint legal custody means that the parties shall share the major decision-making necessary for raising a child such as the child's religion, education, health and extracurricular activities.

Joint physical custody: Parties who share the care of their child equally or nearly equally have joint physical custody of the child.

Judgment: A court order.

Jurisdiction: The legal authority to make judgments. Personal jurisdiction is authority over a person giving the court the authority to order that person to do or not do something. Subject matter jurisdiction is authority over the subject matter of the case such as a family court having jurisdiction over custody cases or a probate court having jurisdiction over wills and administration of estates after someone has died. Although not commonly used, there is also *in rem* jurisdiction which means authority over property such as where a landlord lives in another state and has abandoned his property – the court would have authority to take action to take the property.

Legal custody: The person with legal custody of a child makes the major decisions for that child such as the child's religion, education, health, and extracurricular activities.

Maintenance: Alimony.

Mediation: A form of alternative dispute resolution where a neutral third party tries to help the parties reach an agreement regarding their dispute.

Noncustodial parent: The parent that does not have custody. In the context of child support, it is the parent who has the child less than one-half of the time or, in the case of parents sharing equal time, the parent whose child support obligation would be greater under the child support laws.

Nonparent custodian: A person who has custody of a child who is not that child's parent.

Obligee: In the context of alimony or child support, it is the party being paid.

Obligor: In the context of alimony or child support, it is the party making the payments.

Order: A document from a judge requiring a party to do or not do something or making awards of money, property or custody of a child.

Parenting plan: A plan detailing legal and physical custody of a child along with the various time sharing arrangements with the child, special conditions of custody or visitation, transportation for visitation, contact with the child when he or she is with the other parent (e.g., telephone calls or video calls), a parent's access to a child's records and more.

Parenting time: Time the parent spends with his or her child is parenting time.

Petition: The document that sets forth a party's claim against another party.

Petitioner: The party who is bringing the claim in court against another party or parties.

Physical custody: Physical care of a child. The child lives with the primary custodian. He or she visits or has parenting time with the other parent who may be referred to as the secondary custodian or the noncustodial parent.

Plaintiff: The party who is bringing the claim in court against another party or parties.

GLOSSARY

<u>Presumptive amount of child support</u>: In child support calculations, the presumptive amount of child support is that amount that will be ordered by the court unless a deviation from the presumptive amount is allowed.

<u>Qualified domestic relations order (QDRO)</u>: An order that sets forth how a retirement plan or pension fund will be split by the parties to a divorce. It is a special type of order that must meet specific requirements, or the holder of the retirement plan or pension fund will probably not take the necessary steps to divide the fund or plan.

<u>Request for production of documents and notice to produce</u>: In discovery, one party may ask the other party to produce documents and things to be inspected by the requesting party by use of a document called a Request for Production of Documents and Notice to Produce. A Notice to Product may be used independently of the Request for Production of Documents to require another party to bring the items specified in the Notice to Produce to trial or other times when evidence is relevant.

<u>Respondent</u>: The party who is being sued.

<u>Restraining order</u>: An order restraining a party from doing something such as an order that the other party shall not go to the home or workplace of the first party.

<u>Rule nisi</u>: A court order requiring one or both parties to show cause why the terms of the order should not be made permanent.

<u>Service of process</u>: The act of giving someone legal papers usually a summons or subpoena.

Split custody: A form of custody where one child lives with one parent and another child lives with the other parent.

Spousal support: Alimony.

Subpoena: An order from a court requiring a witness to appear and testify in court or requiring a non-party to produce documents or other evidence in court.

Summons: An order from a court requiring a party to appear in court or answer a complaint.

Uncontested divorce: A divorce where neither party disagrees about any aspect of the divorce.

Uninsured health care expenses: Medical, dental, counseling and similar costs.

Visitation: Time a parent spends with his or her child that is ordered by a court.

www.ingramcontent.com/pod-product-compliance
Lightning Source LLC
Chambersburg PA
CBHW050024230526
45470CB00003B/1116